MAGIC

Written by Felicia Law

Illustrated by Gillian Were

COLLINS   DANDELIONS

London and Glasgow

CONTENTS

Art Director: Sue Tarsky

Educational research by Julia Cleare

General research by Franciska Bayliss

First published in Dandelions 1977
by William Collins Sons and Co Ltd
London and Glasgow
Printed in Great Britain
© 1977 text Felicia Law
© 1977 illustrations William Collins Sons and Co Ltd

THE WITCHDOCTOR

A violent storm rages through the forest. In a clearing, the tribe gathers in front of the witchdoctor's hut, while he performs his tribal dances to frighten away the evil spirits of the storm.

As he leaps and twists, he chants spells in a low mumble or screeches curses at the sky. He wears a terrifying mask and his body is painted with powdered dyes and plant juices. He wears animal skins and bird feathers, and has the bones of dead animals in his hair and ears. Many primitive tribes throughout the world choose one important person to perform the magic for his tribe. This man or woman may be called a witchdoctor, a medicine-man or shaman. They are often more powerful than the tribal chief, because the tribe believes they are in touch with supernatural spirits that control their lives.

SUPERNATURAL SPIRITS

Primitive people understand little about the earth they live on or the world of outer space. They cannot explain why the sun moves across the sky, why thunder roars or why hurricanes blow, except as the work of supernatural spirits. They believe in spirits who control the sun, wind and rain and who live inside animals, plants and trees. Some of the spirits are good and helpful, while others are wicked and may cause harm or bring bad luck.

Since prehistoric times people have tried to influence or control these spirits and the mysterious world of the unknown by practising magic. There are two basic kinds of magic; black magic which is meant to cause harm and white magic which is helpful. People believed to be practising black magic have often been severely punished. White magic includes trying to foretell the future in different ways. This is a form of magic which is still very popular today.

SUPERSTITIONS

Even today, when scientists can explain many things that happen in the world, some people still believe in the power of magic. Our ancestors thought they could control spirits with charms and spells. Some of these have been passed down from generation to generation and have become part of our way of life. Children still sometimes chant this old rhyme, when they see an ambulance pass, to protect themselves from accidents.

Touch collar,
Never swallow,
Never get fever,
Touch your nose,
Touch your toes,
Never get on one of those.

Many old beliefs or superstitions make us behave in certain ways. People walk around a ladder rather than underneath it. There may be some sense in this, but why should it be unlucky to open an umbrella indoors?

Some people throw spilt salt over their left shoulders, wear patched clothes or catch falling leaves to bring them good luck. Others may wear sprigs of white heather in their buttonholes, carry stones with holes in them, or wear locks of hair around their necks.

Old shoes to kick at evil spirits are tied behind the car of a newly-married couple when they leave on their honeymoon. Friends throw confetti over them in hope that the couple will have many children.

6

THE LUCKY HORSESHOE

One of the most famous lucky charms is a horseshoe. A story tells how Saint Dunstan, who was a blacksmith, was visited by a strange-looking customer. The customer asked for a new horseshoe for his foot. When he lifted it up to the anvil, Saint Dunstan recognized the shape of a split, or cloven, hoof. He immediately knew that his customer was the Devil.

He hammered on the horseshoe so roughly that the Devil screamed with pain and begged him to stop. But Saint Dunstan went on hammering mercilessly. He only stopped when the Devil promised that he would never enter a house with a horseshoe nailed over the door.

LUCKY NUMBERS

3 is a very lucky number as it is considered both magical and holy. There are many stories about three heroes who were triplets. In the Bible three angels guard the throne of God. In the East, the third day of the new moon is the luckiest.

4 is the luckiest of the even numbers. It represents the elements: air, earth, fire and water. Finding a four-leafed clover is said to bring you luck.

7 is an especially lucky number in reading tea leaves. It is also a magical number which often appears in fairy tales. The seventh child of the seventh child is said to have special powers to foretell the future.

13 is an unlucky number. The twelve gods of Norse mythology were feasting when the mischievous Loki joined them. He started a quarrel and one of the gods was killed. Perhaps for this reason it is considered bad luck to sit thirteen people at table.

You can calculate your own lucky number. Write down the day, month and year of your birth in numbers (as $16+5+1969$) and add them up (37). Keep adding the digits together until you get a one figure number ($3+7=10$; $1+0=1$). That is your lucky birth number.

MAGIC SQUARES

In a magic square the numbers in all the lines add up to the same total. Add a line across, downwards and diagonally and you will get the same total each time.

The secret number in a magic square is the centre one. Multiply this number by three to get the line totals. Can you find the missing numbers in the square?

To make a magic cube you will need: A piece of strong paper, scissors, a pencil and glue.

Copy the cube shape onto the paper and cut it out. Work out the answers to all the magic squares and write them in. Fold the paper on the dotted lines and glue the tabs to form a cube.

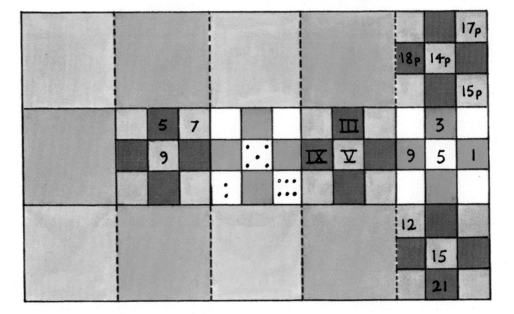

MAGIC SIGNS

The pentangle is a magic sign. It was used in the Middle Ages by astrologers who studied the mysteries of the stars and planets. It was marked over doorways as a charm to keep away witches and evil spirits.

The pentangle is made up of five straight lines formed into a five-pointed star. Try to draw it without taking your pencil off the paper.

Here is a magical alphabet. The signs are said to have special magical powers. Write your name using the signs instead of letters.

A	B	C	D	E	F	G	H	I
Y	൜	∿	⊕	⋀	Ψ	X	⬗	△

J	K	L	M	N	O	P	Q	R
⌄	◨	⤬	☾	⊢	♂	♃	♄	ℕ

S	T	U	V	W	X	Y	Z
⩜	♉	⊓	⅍	⋀	⚹	♅	♇

WITCHES

Wise men and women were sometimes thought to be wizards and witches. They seemed to understand the mysteries of nature, the weather and the countryside. They mixed powdered herbs and flowers into medicines to cure sickness. They chanted spells to grant people's wishes, and predicted what was going to happen.

Although people were frightened of witches and wizards, they respected the magical powers. Exaggerated stories described how witches flew through the night sky on broomsticks, or cursed cattle so that they sickened. Witches were even said to make dead people come to life again!

MAKE A MODEL WITCH

You will need: A washing-up liquid container weighted with a few clean pebbles, pipecleaners, paper handkerchiefs, an old mixing bowl and spoon, a packet of Polyfilla, water, rubber bands, paints and brushes, spray varnish, cardboard and scissors.

1

Join two pipecleaners together and wrap them firmly around the container a little way from the top to form arms for the witch's body. Attach other pipecleaners to these to make fingers.

2

Mix 4 heaped tablespoons of Polyfilla with 4 tablespoons of water in the bowl. Stir well with the spoon until you have a smooth paste.

3

Dip each paper handkerchief into the mixture and drape it over the container and the arms to form a loose gown. Wrap handkerchiefs around the top of the container to make a face with hooked nose and ears. Twist handkerchiefs into long straggly hair.

Cut out a triangular-shaped piece of cardboard and roll it up to form a pointed hat. Glue firmly and set into a circular crown made from a ring of cardboard.

Fix the hat on the head by wrapping handkerchiefs around the brim and draping them over the pointed cone.

Let the model dry. Paint it with bright colours. Spray it with varnish for a shiny hard coating.

CAST A MAGIC SPELL

You will need: A sheet of white paper, silver and gold foil scraps, scissors, glue, felt pens and cold coffee or tea to use as a stain.
Make up a spell using magical words, nonsense words, and names of strange animals, plants and magic spirits. Print the spell on the paper. Decorate it with cut-out pictures of moons, stars, witches' hats, cats' eyes and magical signs. Brush the edges of the paper with cold tea or coffee. Wrinkle the paper to make your spell look ancient and mysterious.

MERLIN

Storytellers have been writing about Arthur, Guinevere and the
Knights of the Round Table since the Dark Ages well over one
thousand years ago. Arthur's adviser was the powerful wizard Merlin.

There was a tradition that whoever pulled the magic sword out of a
great stone would be king. When all the other Knights had failed,
Arthur removed the sword with the aid of Merlin's magic, to become
King of England and Wales.

Legend says that Merlin placed Stonehenge where it stands today.
Arthur's father, King Uther, wished to honour the burial ground of his
knights killed in battle. Merlin sailed to Ireland to find the Giant's
Ring, a huge circle of tall standing stones. Using his magic, he
collapsed the stones, lifted them on board his ship, and set them up
again on Salisbury Plain in the south of England.

FAMILIARS

Witches and wizards kept familiars, or animal pets, to help them with their spells or to spy out information. Familiars had magical powers of their own, too. They could talk like humans, make themselves invisible, or turn into grisly shapes to frighten away enemies.

The most common familiars were black cats with shiny coats and glinting eyes. Other familiars were slimy toads, moles, sharp-eyed ferrets, spiders, weasels, rats and mice. Some were birds like the jackdaw and the owl, who were thought to be sly, mean or wise, like their masters.

Strange familiars were made of mixtures of different animals. One might have the head of a lion, the hooves of a goat and the wings of a bird. Paint a picture of a weird familiar using parts of many animals.

SOME MAGIC CURES

Here are some cures that people used long ago.

A Wart on your Hand:
Rub your hand in the moon's rays as it shines
in a dry metal basin and recite,
"I wash my hands in this thy dish
O man in the moon, do grant my wish,
And come and take away this."

Nettle Stings:
Rub with a dock leaf, chanting,
"Nettle out, dock in.
Dock remove the nettle sting."

A Toothache:
Wear a dead mole around your neck.

Write ABRACADABRA like this on a piece
of paper and wear it round your neck
to ward off a fever!

THE MAGIC CAULDRON

As the witches chanted their spells, they threw strange objects into the bubbling cauldrons. Their brews might include sticky cobwebs, lizards' tails, hedgehog prickles or dragons' teeth.

Mix your own hissing, steaming potion with these ingredients:
3 teaspoonfuls bicarbonate of soda and $\frac{1}{4}$ cup of vinegar.

Watch it bubble and listen to it hiss, but DON'T DRINK the mixture!

Play this game with your friends.

Fill a large cooking pot with a damp sponge for a giant's tongue, a shelled hard-boiled egg for a dragon's eye, broken shells for dragon scales and cold, cooked macaroni for serpents' tails.

Blindfold friends one at a time and ask them to remove a particular imaginary object from the pot. Give them ten seconds to find it.

DEVILS AND DEMONS

Devils and demons are powerful evil spirits. In Europe, devils were thought to have forked tails, pointed ears and cloven feet like goats' hooves. They often worked with witches to perform black magic. In the Middle Ages, one expert claimed that there were 1,758,064,176 devils at work in the world!

Ancient Persians, Hindus, Chinese and Japanese believed in demons of the underworld. In Japan the demons called Oni had red or green bodies with heads of oxen or horses. They drove fiery chariots to take away wicked people to the underworld. The gaki demons had huge bellies and were constantly tormented by hunger and thirst. They could take the shape of people or things to do their wicked deeds. Other demons were invisible but could be spotted by their singing, whistling and talking.

Make up a devil or demon of your own. Paint a picture of it doing some mischief. Invent a name for it such as 'Durtideed' or 'Wotapest'.

MAGICAL CREATURES

For centuries, people believed that small magical people shared their homes and countryside. These small, elf-like people were teasing and mischievous. They were often blamed for accidents, for making startling noises and for causing frights and surprises. The tiny people are described differently in almost every country of the world.

Irish leprechauns are said to wear green clothes. Like pixies, elves and imps, they play tricks on humans. They may blow out candles on dark stairs, make frightening noises in walls or lead travellers astray across bogs and moors.

Scandinavian legends tell of the ugly, hunchbacked trolls who live in the dark forests, and who turn to stone instantly if they see the sun.

The bunyip is a legendary water monster, half reptile and half mammal, that lurks in the muddy waterholes and lagoons of the Australian outback. It lures its victims into the dark water with its glowing eyes. On moonlight nights it sometimes rises to the surface and utters bloodcurdling moans, warning all creatures to keep away.

Giants were supposed to be huge magical people, blamed for rock falls, floods and wild storms. In Northern Ireland, six-sided rocks have been thrown up by the volcanic eruptions below the Earth's surface. The rocks lie neatly arranged in steps. The people who lived there believed that a group of giants had once built these, and so they called the steps the Giant's Causeway.

FAIRIES

Superstitious people say that a circle of worn grass or a ring of mushrooms mark the spot where fairies dance at their midnight revels. They warn you not to step inside the ring as you might be pinched black and blue or carried off to fairyland. Spiteful fairies may exchange their elfin babies for human children. Without knowing it, the human mothers rear these changelings, until one day they suddenly notice their children have pointed ears and tiny sprouting wings!

In fairy tales, fairies reward people who are good and generous. A woman who places a saucer of milk on her doorstep will find her housework done in the morning. Children who bravely pull out wobbly teeth will find that the fairies have placed a silver coin under their pillows when they wake in the morning.

DRAGONS, AND UNICORNS

When the huge, fossilized bones of dinosaurs were first unearthed, many people believed that these were the remains of dragons. However, dragons are imaginary creatures. They were first mentioned in stories told long ago when they were described as magical lizards. In later tales they became fierce monsters with huge wings, sharp claws, scaly bodies and nostrils that belched fire and smoke.

The red, black and white striped horn of the unicorn was supposed to be magical. Some believed that cups and spoons made of unicorn horn could make a poisonous drink harmless. In the French court in 1800, the king's food was still tested with 'unicorn horn' forks. It is more likely that the horn came from a rhinoceros.

THE DELPHIC ORACLE

The prophetess sat on a three-legged stool, chewing quietly and thoughtfully from a plate of laurel leaves. Grouped around her, silent and stern, stood the priests of the city of Delphi in Greece. As she muttered strange words, the priests listened carefully, trying hard to understand her meaning. They believed she was able to speak for the god Apollo.

The Greek rulers asked her advice on many important matters, and trusted her to tell exactly what was in store for them. Often her answers were vague, and her advice could either be taken to mean one thing, or quite the opposite. For many hundreds of years one prophetess after another held the important position of fortune-teller or oracle at Delphi.

24

THE FORTUNE-TELLER

In one corner of the fairground stands a small tent. The doorway flap is closed but across the entrance hangs a painted sign saying, *Madame Mystique, gypsy fortune-teller*. The queue of waiting customers hope she has the power to predict their futures.

One at a time, people go into her dark tent. Inside, they see the gypsy woman sitting at a table. She wears a fringed headscarf and shawl, and gold earrings dangle from her ears. She beckons customers to sit down at the table, and gazes deeply into a crystal ball in front of her. She seems to see moving pictures, shapes and words hidden in the glass. Slowly, she explains their mysterious meanings. She recalls things that happened long ago to her customer, and foretells events to come.

PALMISTRY

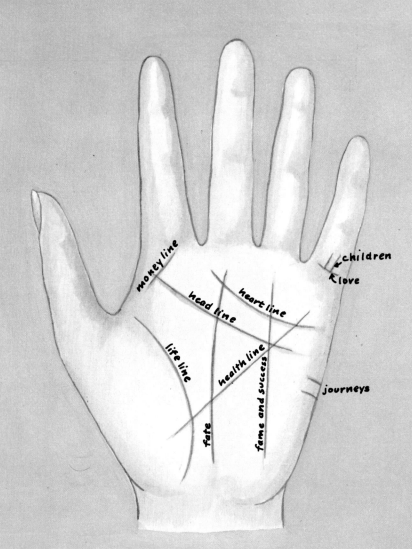

The palms of your hands are criss-crossed with lines and the gypsy fortune-teller may try to predict your future by looking at them. Everybody has different patterns on their palms and fingers but very few hands have all the lines shown. If you are right-handed the palmist reads your right hand to see what you will make of your life, while your left hand shows the possibilities with which you were born. If you are left-handed it is exactly the reverse. Palmistry is a very ancient art which was practised in the Far East at least five thousand years ago.

CARD READING

All cards can be used for fortune-telling, but sometimes a special pack called the Tarot is used. Tarot cards are supposed to be especially magical and their origin is ancient and mysterious.

There are 78 cards in the Tarot pack. 56 of them are divided into four suits: Wands, Cups, Swords and Pentacles, or Coins, with an extra court card, the knight. The other 22 are special trump cards with strange pictures on them which can have many different meanings.

There are many ways of using a Tarot pack. One of them is to tell the future by using the Clock, or Circle, spread method. 12 cards are laid down in a circle and a 13th is placed in the middle. Card 13 is read first as a forecast for the whole year; then the others are read one by one. If the cards are laid upside down their meanings change.

27

ASTROLOGY

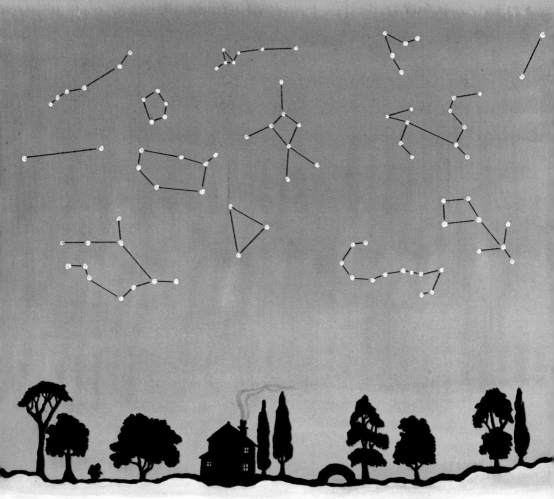

For thousands of years, people looking at the night sky have seen patterns in the stars. Astrologers believe that these patterns hold a message. They have named the belt of stars that lie in the sun's path, the Zodiac. The belt is divided into twelve sections and each section has a Zodiac sign and name.

Astrologers believe that the positions of the stars and planets at a person's birth can explain their character. If you want to know about your personality, you must give the astrologer the date, place and exact time of your birth.

Which is your Zodiac sign? What can you find out about people who are born under your sign?

28

STAGE MAGIC

The earliest recorded magician was Tchatcha-em-ankh, who performed magic tricks at the court of King Khufu of Egypt in 3766 BC. Since then, magicians all over the world have performed what seems to be magic as entertainment.

In India, men dressed in long robes squat in the market place, charming snakes out of baskets and sending small boys up ropes suspended in the air. Chinese magicians walk on fire or climb ladders made of razor-sharp swords.

Modern magicians use many ancient tricks. Conjuring is a matter of practice and no magical powers are needed. A conjuror must perform his tricks so skilfully that the audience are completely baffled by his movements. Often he tries to distract their attention with jokes and chatter while his fingers are preparing some trick.

HOUDINI

Harry Houdini was a famous American conjuror. His success began when he discovered that very few people can tie a really tight knot, and that handcuffs spring open when they are banged against a wall in a certain way. He trained hard to become fit and strong, and practised breath and muscle control. Ropes that held him firmly when his chest was puffed up and his muscles were tight, slipped off easily when he relaxed his body.

For three hours, Houdini kept his audience spellbound. He challenged them to lock him in chains and handcuffs, tie him in a sack, and padlock him into a trunk, which was then lowered into a tank of water. As the minutes dragged on and on, the audience grew breathless with suspense. Finally they became so restless that they shouted for the trunk to be raised. At that moment, Houdini climbed from the trunk, calm and smiling.

30

THE CONJUROR

The conjuror asks the audience to tie his wrists together using the ends of a long length of string. While this is going on, he hands a bracelet to the audience and asks them to make sure it cannot be opened in any way. When his wrists are tied, he turns his back quickly on the audience, and saying 'Abracadabra', he faces them with the bracelet dangling from the string.

Try this trick for yourself while wearing long sleeves.
You will need: A length of string, about 50 cms long, and 2 identical bracelets large enough to slip over your wrists.
Slide one bracelet up your arm and hide it under your sleeve. When you turn your back to the audience, slip the bracelet the audience has examined into your pocket and slide the other one down your arm and on to the string.

THE KINGS GO ON HOLIDAY

Mystify your friends with this magic card trick.

You will need: A pack of cards without the jokers.

Take out the four Kings and any other two cards you choose. Fan out the four Kings in your hand, carefully hiding the other two cards behind the Kings. Show your audience the four Kings.

Close the fan, making sure that the two cards you chose are now on top of the kings.

Place these two cards in the centre of the pack, saying, "The King of Spades and the King of Clubs are going on holiday."

Hold two of the remaining Kings together to look like one card. Place them on the bottom of the pack, saying, "The King of Hearts is going on holiday."

Hold the two remaining Kings together to look like one card. Place them on top of the pack, saying, "The King of Diamonds is going on holiday."

Cut the pack, which puts all the kings together.

Thumb through the pack in front of your audience, saying, "The Kings have decided to meet for their holiday," as you come across the four Kings together!